Reproducible!

Instant BIBLE LESSONS® For PRETEENS

Equipped For Life

Mary J. Davis

These pages may be copied.
Permission is granted to the buyer of this book to photocopy student materials for use with Sunday school or Bible teaching classes.

ROSEKIDZ®
An imprint of Rose Publishing, Inc.
Carson, CA
www.Rose-Publishing.com

To my husband, Larry. To Jeff, Pam, Wendi, Lori, Kirk, and all our eight grandchildren.

INSTANT BIBLE LESSONS® FOR PRETEENS: EQUIPPED FOR LIFE

ISBN 10: 1-58411-076-7
ISBN 13: 978-1-58411-076-7
RoseKidz® reorder# R38613
RELIGION / Christian Ministry / Youth

RoseKidz®
An imprint of Rose Publishing, Inc.
17909 Adria Maru Lane
Carson, CA 90746
www.Rose-Publishing.com

Cover Illustrator: Jennifer Kalis
Interior Illustrator: Apryl Stott

Printed in the United States of America *10 05.2016.PP*

Contents

Introduction

Let's face it: the preteen years are a struggle. Bodily changes, emotional highs and lows, and hormones run amok are just some of the challenges of this age. The world bombards our preteens with unsavory messages at every turn. They need encouragement and opportunity to put God's Word into their hearts and minds. The best tools we can give our preteens to help them survive in the world today are God's Holy Word and our guidance. In ***Equipped For Life***, preteens will learn how the fundamental truths of the Bible equip them to handle life's challenges, both great and small.

Each of the first eight chapters includes a Bible story, a memory verse, alternative forms of learning the lesson theme, and a variety of activities to help reinforce the truth in the lesson. The ninth chapter contains miscellaneous projects that can be used anytime throughout the study, or at the end to review the lessons.

The most exciting aspect of ***Instant Bible Lessons for Preteens*** is its flexibility. You can easily adapt these lessons to a Sunday school hour, a children's church service, a Wednesday night Bible study, or family home use. Because there is a variety of reproducible ideas from which to choose, you will enjoy creating a class session that is best for your group of students, whether large or small, beginning or advanced, active or studious, all boys/all girls/co-ed. The intriguing topics will keep your students coming back for more, week after week.

* How to Use This Book *

Each chapter begins with a Bible story. You may simply tell the story from the story page, or use the first activity to discover the lesson in a more involved way. To prepare for each lesson, duplicate the story page. Read the Bible Scriptures and the story written on the page to get a good background of the lesson you will teach your students. Jot down any thoughts that will help you teach the Bible story. Use the discussion questions to spark conversation.

bulletin board

craft

express yourself

game

group

song

puzzle

skit

teacher help

think

Car Mirror Hanger

Ten Commandments

Exodus 20: 1 - 17

I am the Lord your God

Exodus 20: 1

finished craft

You shall have no other gods before me

You shall not make for yourself an idol

You shall not misuse the name of the Lord your God

Remember the Sabbath Day by keeping it holy

Honor your father and mother

You shall not murder

You shall not commit adultery

You shall not steal

You shall not give false testimony against your neighbor

You shall not covet

craft

WHAT YOU NEED

- duplicated page
- plastic breath mint boxes
- scissors
- embroidery thread, various colors
- hot/cool glue guns
- ruler
- tape

WHAT TO DO

1. Before class peel the labels from the mint boxes (or have the students do it, if time allows). Use warm water and wash cloths to remove the remainder of the labels. (Fingernail polish remover and cotton balls will also help remove the sticky substance.) You will need two boxes per student.
2. Have each student cut out the four rectangles.
3. Show how to put one of the rectangles inside a box, printed side facing out (use a ruler end to push the paper against the side of the box securely).
4. Using the same ➢

WHAT TO DO, CONTINUED

➢ box, show how to put one of the two verse rectangles inside the opposite side of the box, with the printed side facing outward.

5. Have the students repeat this with their second boxes, using the other rectangles.
6. Cut a two-foot length of embroidery thread from each of three different colors for each student. Show how to tape the top ends of the three lengths together and braid them.
7. Have the students tape the bottoms of their braids to hold them.
8. Go around and use a glue gun to attach the ends of each student's braid to the tops of his or her boxes.
9. Say, **You can hang your Ten Commandments over the mirror in your parents' car or on a hook in your room, or attach them to your backpack.**

song

WHAT YOU NEED

- duplicated page

WHAT TO DO

1. Have the students sing the song to the tune of "10 Little Indians."
2. Do a commandment countdown using the song sheets by shouting out the numbers from one to ten and having the students answer with that numbered commandment.

Commandments Song

Have no other gods
is the first commandment,
Have no other gods
is the first commandment,
Have no other gods
is the first commandment,
For I am the Lord your God.

Don't have any idols
is the second commandment,
Don't have any idols
is the second commandment,
Don't have any idols
is the second commandment,
For I am the Lord your God.

Don't misuse God's name
is the third commandment,
Don't misuse God's name
is the third commandment,
Don't misuse God's name
is the third commandment,
For I am the Lord your God.

Make the Sabbath holy
is the fourth commandment,
Make the Sabbath holy
is the fourth commandment,
Make the Sabbath holy
is the fourth commandment,
For I am the Lord your God.

Honor your father and mother
is the fifth commandment,
Honor your father and mother
is the fifth commandment,
Honor your father and mother
is the fifth commandment,
For I am the Lord your God.

You shall not murder
is the sixth commandment,
You shall not murder
is the sixth commandment,
You shall not murder
is the sixth commandment,
For I am the Lord your God.

Don't commit adultery
is the seventh commandment,
Don't commit adultery
is the seventh commandment,
Don't commit adultery
is the seventh commandment,
For I am the Lord your God.

You shall not steal
is the eighth commandment,
You shall not steal
is the eighth commandment,
You shall not steal
is the eighth commandment,
For I am the Lord your God.

Don't give false witness
is the ninth commandment,
Don't give false witness
is the ninth commandment,
Don't give false witness
is the ninth commandment,
For I am the Lord your God.

Don't covet stuff
is the tenth commandment,
Don't covet stuff
is the tenth commandment,
Don't covet stuff
is the tenth commandment,
For I am the Lord your God.

CHAPTER 2

The 23rd Psalm

MEMORY VERSE

The Lord is my shepherd, I shall not be in want. PSALM 23:1

* Filled to Overflowing *

The 23rd Psalm is one of the 150 psalms, and perhaps the most well-known. Most of the psalms were written by David. Sometimes David was filled with joy and thankfulness for everything that God provided. Other times, David had sin in his life, and was grateful for God's forgiveness. David also was afraid of his enemies and asked for God's help. God knew that David's psalms could help all people. That's why He inspired David to write the psalms, and why He wanted the psalms in the Bible.

Let's look at each of the verses from Psalm 23:

Verse 1 says, "The Lord is my shepherd, I shall not be in want." God wants us to know that He always protects us, just as a shepherd cares for his sheep. We have all we need.

Verse 2 says, "He makes me lie down in green pastures, He leads me beside quiet waters." This tells us that God gives us great peace.

Verse 3 tells us, "He restores my soul. He guides me in the paths of righteousness for his name's sake." God guides us in ways that will help us not to sin.

Verse 4 says, "Even though I walk through the valley of the shadow of death, I will fear no evil, for you are with me; Your rod and your staff, they comfort me." God wants you to know that He is with us, bringing us comfort and help.

Verse 5 says, "You prepare a table before me in the presence of my enemies. You anoint my head with oil; my cup overflows." God takes care of us and helps us have victory over our enemies. He also gives us many more blessings than an evil person ever sees.

Verse 6 says, "Surely goodness and love will follow me all the days of my life, and I will dwell in the house of the Lord forever." Isn't it rewarding to study hard and get an A on a test at school? How much more rewarding it is when you know you have tried hard to obey God and be good for Him! And, yes, there is a reward. You will dwell in God's House—heaven—forever and ever!

BASED ON PSALM 23

Discussion Questions

1. Why do you think David wrote psalms to tell about God?
2. If you could write a psalm about God, what would you say?

skit

WHAT YOU NEED

- pages 19 and 20, duplicated
- props (listed)

WHAT TO DO

1. Before class, gather all the props.
2. Give each student a skit page. Designate a student to read and use a prop for each of the verses. If your class is small, have some students read more than one part. If your class is large, have one student read the part while another holds up the prop.
3. Place the props on a table in front of the students who will be using them.
4. Have the students read their lines and hold up the props to match their lines.
5. Do the skit more than once if the students are enjoying it.
6. If the skit goes well, consider performing it for another class.

23rd Psalm

* Silly Props Skit *

Props

toy sheep or picture of sheep

cotton stuffing

basketful of food or bread loaf

green tissue paper

glass of water and extra glass

plain paper arrow that says “This Way”

dark towel or blanket

paper plate with “fear” crossed out on it

wood or cardboard cane

dinner plate and silverware

bottle or jar of oil

cup overflowing with cotton balls or packing peanuts

red construction paper heart

calendar

picture of clouds and picture of a church

The 23rd Psalm

The Lord is my shepherd, [*hold cotton to chin for a shepherd's beard, them hold up a toy sheep or a picture of a sheep*]

I shall not be in want. [*hold up basket of food or loaf of bread*]

He makes me lie down in green pastures, [*wrinkle up green tissue paper and lay head on paper as though resting*]

he leads me beside quiet waters, [*pour water from one glass to another*]

he restores my soul.

He guides me in the paths of righteousness for his name's sake. [*hold up "This Way" arrow*]

Even though I walk through the valley of the shadow of death,

I will fear no evil, [*pass dark towel or blanket in front of face]*

for you are with me. [*hold up paper plate with "no fear" on it*]

Your rod and your staff, they comfort me. [*hold up cane or cardboard staff*]

You prepare a table before me in the presence of my enemies. [*hold up a plate and silverware*]

You anoint my head with oil; [*hold up a jar of oil*]

my cup overflows. [*hold up filled cup, tip a little to be 'overflowing' with the cotton or packing peanuts*]

Surely goodness and love [*hold up paper heart*]

will follow me all the days of my life, [*hold up calendar*]

and I will dwell in the house of the Lord forever. [*hold up picture of church and picture of clouds*]

bulletin board

WHAT YOU NEED

- duplicated page
- markers or colored pencils
- heavy-weight cardboard, 9" x 12"
- embroidery floss, yarn scraps, or cord, bright colors
- tape
- scissors

WHAT TO DO

1. Give each student a 9" x 12" piece of cardboard.
2. Have each student use a ruler to mark a 1½" frame around the edge.
3. Have the students use scissors to carefully cut out the centers, leaving only the frames.
4. Have the students choose one or more colors of floss, yarn, or cord. Show how to tape one end of the floss to the back of the frame, and wrap the floss around the 1½" edge of the frame, keeping the floss close together to cover the cardboard. ➢

23rd Psalm

* Verse Poster *

The 23rd Psalm

The Lord is my shepherd, I shall not be in want. He makes me lie down in green pastures, He leads me beside quiet waters, He restores my soul. He guides me in the paths of righteousness for his name's sake. Even though I walk through the valley of the shadow of death, I will fear no evil, for you are with me; Your rod and your staff, they comfort me. You prepare a table before me in the presence of my enemies. You anoint my head with oil; my cup overflows. Surely goodness and love will follow me all the days of my life, and I will dwell in the house of the Lord forever.

WHAT TO DO, CONTINUED

5. ➢ Each student should continue to wrap until his or her entire frame is covered (each new color of floss should be taped to the backs of the frames in order to continue wrapping until the frames are covered).
6. When the frames are finished, the students should tape their posters to the backs so the printed sides of their posters show through the frames. Show how to tape a loop of yarn or floss to the top of the frame for a hanger.

Painted Window Block

The Lord is my shepherd, I shall not be in want. He makes me lie down in green pastures, he leads me beside quiet waters, he restores my soul. He guides me in paths of righteousness for his name's sake.

Even though I walk through the valley of the shadow of death, I will fear no evil, for you are with me; your rod and your staff, they comfort me. You prepare a table before me in the presence of my enemies. You anoint my head with oil; my cup overflows.

Surely goodness and love will follow me all the days of my life, and I will dwell in the house of the Lord forever. ***Psalm 23***

finished craft

Note: You can buy glass window blocks at home improvement stores. Or, substitute framed mirrors or blocks of wood for the window blocks.

craft

WHAT YOU NEED

- duplicated page
- glass window blocks
- glass paint
- paintbrushes
- glue
- scissors

WHAT TO DO

1. Give each student a duplicated page and a window block.
2. Have the students cut the verse strips from their pages and glue the strips on three sides of their window blocks.
3. Let each student use glass paint to write "The Lord is my shepherd" on an empty side of a window block. Suggest that they add designs to the other blank sides of their blocks.
4. Say, **Isn't it a great comfort to read this Psalm and know that God has provided for all our needs?**

puzzle

WHAT YOU NEED

- pages 22 and 23, duplicated
- pens or pencils
- Bibles

WHAT TO DO

1. Give each student a crossword puzzle page.
2. Have the students write the correct words in the blanks. The students can use their Bibles to find the correct words.
3. After they fill in the blanks, have the students use those words to fill in their crossword puzzles.

23rd Psalm

* Crossword Psalm *

Across

2. Surely goodness and _ _ _ _ (vs. 6)
4. The Lord is my _ _ _ _ _ _ _ _ (vs. 1)
7. Will _ _ _ _ _ _ me all the days of my life (vs. 6)
10. Your _ _ _ and your staff (vs. 4)
11. He _ _ _ _ _ _ me in paths of righteousness (vs. 3)
12. He leads me beside quiet _ _ _ _ _ _ (vs. 2)
13. And I will dwell in the house of the Lord _ _ _ _ _ _ _ (vs. 6)
14. He makes me lie down in green _ _ _ _ _ _ _ _ (vs. 2)
17. Your rod and your _ _ _ _ _ (vs. 4)
18. In the presence of my _ _ _ _ _ _ _ (vs. 5)
19. Surely _ _ _ _ _ _ _ _ and love (vs. 6)
21. Even though I walk through the _ _ _ _ _ _ (vs. 4)
23. He restores my _ _ _ _ (vs. 3)

Down

1. My cup _ _ _ _ _ _ _ _ _ (vs. 5)
3. You prepare a _ _ _ _ _ before me (vs. 5)
5. And I will dwell in the _ _ _ _ _ (vs. 6)
6. Paths of _ _ _ _ _ _ _ _ _ _ _ _ _ (vs. 3)
8. I shall not be in _ _ _ _ (vs. 1)
9. You anoint my head with _ _ _ (vs. 5)
15. Of the _ _ _ _ _ _ of death (vs. 4)
16. For his _ _ _ _ 's sake (vs. 3)
20. I will fear no _ _ _ _ for you are with me (vs. 4)
22. I will dwell in the house of the _ _ _ _ forever (vs. 6)

1
2
3
4
5
6
7
8
9
10
11
12
13
14
15
16
17
18
19
20
21
22
23

craft

WHAT YOU NEED

- duplicated page
- markers
- button maker or button kit
- scissors

WHAT TO DO

1. Give each student a pattern page. If you don't have a button maker or kit, use cardboard and pin backings.
2. Allow each student to cut out at least one button pattern, then use markers to decorate the buttons as they wish.
3. Follow the directions on the button maker or kit. If you use cardboard, have the students glue the circles to cardboard and trim. Go around and hot glue a pin backing or safety pin to the back of each circle.
4. Say, **When we wear our Psalm 23 buttons, we are reminded that God provides all we need: food, shelter, guidance, care, and even an everlasting home in heaven.**

23rd Psalm

Psalm 23 Buttons

The Lord
is my
SHEPHERD

My Cup
OVERFLOWS

I will
fear no evil,
for you are
with me

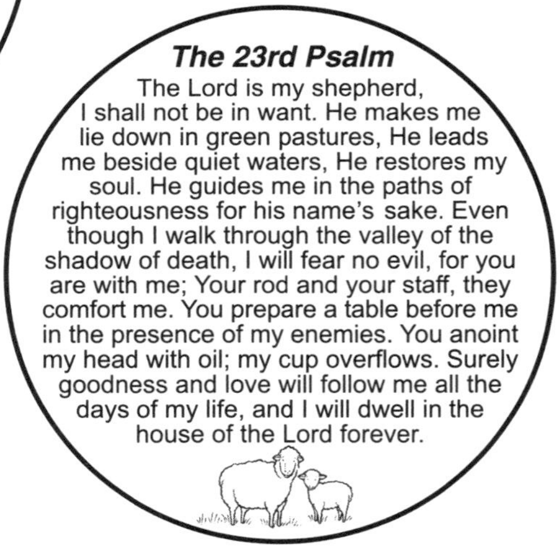
The 23rd Psalm
The Lord is my shepherd,
I shall not be in want. He makes me
lie down in green pastures, He leads
me beside quiet waters, He restores my
soul. He guides me in the paths of
righteousness for his name's sake. Even
though I walk through the valley of the
shadow of death, I will fear no evil, for you
are with me; Your rod and your staff, they
comfort me. You prepare a table before me
in the presence of my enemies. You anoint
my head with oil; my cup overflows. Surely
goodness and love will follow me all the
days of my life, and I will dwell in the
house of the Lord forever.

Construct-a-Verse

—*The 23rd Psalm*

The Lord is my shepherd.

I shall not be in want.

He makes me lie down in green pastures,

He leads me beside quiet waters,

He restores my soul.

He guides me in paths of righteousness for his name's sake.

Even though I walk through the valley of the shadow of death,

I will fear no evil,

For you are with me;

Your rod and your staff,

They comfort me.

You prepare a table before me

In the presence of my enemies.

You anoint my head with oil;

My cup overflows.

Surely goodness and love

Will follow me all the days of my life,

And I will dwell in the house of the Lord forever.

game

WHAT YOU NEED

- duplicated page
- scissors

WHAT TO DO

1. Before class, cut the verse sections from the pages, one set per team.
2. Divide the class into teams.
3. Have each team stand around a table.
4. Place the verse pieces in front of each team.
5. On "go," each team should put the verse pieces together in order to construct the verse.
6. Give a reward to all the students for participating.

23rd Psalm

express yourself

WHAT YOU NEED

- duplicated page
- pens or pencils

WHAT TO DO

1. Give each student a journal page.
2. Say, **The 23rd Psalm tells us that God cares for our every need. What a wonderful thought to keep in our minds! Use this journal page to thank God for His care. You can also write about some times when you especially felt God caring for you.**

23rd Psalm

* God's Care * Journal Page

God Cares for Me

Psalm 23

Thank You, God...

____

____

____

____

____

____

____

I truly feel God's care for me when...

____

____

____

____

____

____

____

The Meaning of All

1. [*bags of marshmallows*] Give each student a handful of marshmallows. Say, **Eat all the marshmallows as quickly as you can.**
2. [*paper and pencils for each student*] Say, **I will count down 15 seconds. Try to write all the letters of the alphabet in fifteen seconds.**
3. [*bags of unpopped corn and a basket for each team of 3 or 4 students. Pour the popcorn onto the table next to each basket*] Say, **Get into teams of 3 (or 4 or 5). When I say, "Go," pick up one popcorn kernel at a time, and put it in the basket. Work as a team to put all the kernels into the basket one at a time.**
4. [*no props needed*] Have the class say the memory verse, Deuteronomy 6:5, together at once.
5. [*10 or more index cards for each pair of students*] Say, **When I say, "Go," begin building a house with the index cards. If your house falls, start over. Use all the cards to build a house.**
6. [*a half-sheet of plain paper for each student, and shallow pans of chocolate or strawberry syrup*] Say, **Stand around the table so that you can each reach a pan of syrup. When I say, "Go," dip one finger into the syrup and then press it onto the paper. Cover all of your paper with fingerprints.**
7. [*no props needed*] Have the students make two teams, then take off their shoes and place them in a pile in the center of an open area. The students should back away from the pile. Say, **When I say, "Go," rush to the pile and get your shoes. The first team with all their shoes back on wins.**
8. [*a 15-foot long rope*] Choose two rope-turners. Have the rest of the class try to jump rope all at once.
9. [*Bibles with Table of Contents pages*] Say, **Get into groups where you can each see the Bible easily. Say all the books of the Bible aloud together.**
10. [*a bag or box of empty cans for the class or teams*] Say, **On "Go," remove the cans from the box [bag] and stack all of the cans. If any fall, you must start over.**

group

WHAT YOU NEED

- duplicated page
- items listed

WHAT TO DO

1. Before class, choose the activities you plan to use.
2. Place items for each activity where you plan to conduct it.
3. Say, **God commands that we love him with all our heart, soul and strength. We are going to do several activities that will help us understand the meaning of "all."**

Commandment

group

WHAT YOU NEED

- duplicated page
- glue
- poster paper
- Bibles
- concordances
- markers

WHAT TO DO

1. Spread the poster paper onto a table or floor so the students can work together. Glue the heading (duplicated page) onto the top of the mural, close to the center.
2. Say, **Let's look up verses that tell us to love God with all our hearts, souls, minds, and strength. Write the references and verses.**
3. Say, **You also can decorate the mural with markers. Let's fasten it to our wall to remind us to love God with all our heart, soul, mind, and strength.** Suggest students draw hearts, make designs, write the word "all," etc.

Commandment

* Love God Mural *

Love the Lord your God with all your heart and with all your soul and with all your mind.

Matthew 22:37

• CHAPTER 4 •

The Beatitudes

MEMORY VERSE

Rejoice and be glad, because great is your reward in heaven.
MATTHEW 5:12

* The Right Attitudes *

Jesus had a wonderful ministry of teaching God's truths and showing God's power through healing the sick. Everywhere Jesus went, crowds of people followed Him.

One day, when Jesus saw the crowds coming toward Him, He went up on a mountainside and sat down. The people gathered near Him to listen to Him teach. Here is what He said:

"Blessed are the poor in spirit, for theirs is the kingdom of heaven. Blessed are those who mourn, for they will be comforted. Blessed are the meek, for they will inherit the earth. Blessed are those who hunger and thirst for righteousness, for they will be filled. Blessed are the merciful, for they will be shown mercy. Blessed are the pure in heart, for they will see God. Blessed are the peacemakers, for they will be called sons of God. Blessed are those who are persecuted because of righteousness, for theirs is the kingdom of heaven."

Jesus continued with blessings for those who follow Him. "Blessed are you when people insult you, persecute you, and falsely say all kinds of evil against you because of Me," He said. "Rejoice and be glad, because great is your reward in heaven, for in the same way they persecuted the prophets who were before you."

Jesus had a special blessing for every situation His followers might encounter in their lives. These blessings, called "The Beatitudes," also could be called "the beautiful attitudes." If we have these beautiful attitudes, our lives will be great witnesses to others. And Jesus promises us great rewards in heaven!

BASED ON MATTHEW 5:3-12

Discussion Questions

1. Why do you think Jesus told people about these blessings for specific situations?
2. Which blessing means the most to you in your life? Why?

puzzle

beatitudes

WHAT YOU NEED

- duplicated page
- pens or pencils
- Bibles or verse

WHAT TO DO

1. Give each student a puzzle page.
2. Say, **Each word in the puzzle has a missing letter. Fill in the letters to find words from the Beatitudes. Then write the missing letters on the blanks below the puzzle. Unscramble the letters to discover Jesus' role in this lesson in addition to being a healer.**

* Jesus, Healer and... *

M __ E K

M O U __ N

P E __ C E M A K E R S

S P I R I __

P U R E I N H __ A R T

__ U N G E R A N D T H I R S T

M E R __ I F U L

__ __ __ __ __ __ __

____

* Mini Skits *

1
I do not boast about my spiritual life. I know I need to walk with God through prayer and Bible study.
Read Matthew 5:3

2
I am mourning for a loved one who has died. I am sad because things in my life have gone wrong.
Read Matthew 5:4

3
I know God is in charge. I do not take His power for granted.
Read Matthew 5:5

group

WHAT YOU NEED

- pages 37 and 38, duplicated
- card stock
- scissors
- Bibles

WHAT TO DO

1. Before class, duplicate the cards on card stock and cut them out.
2. Divide the class into eight pairs. If you have a small class, each student can do both parts of a skit.
3. Give each pair of students a card and a Bible. Say, **Find Matthew 5:3-12 in your Bibles so you are ready for the skit.**
4. Have one student in the first pair read the card to explain "who" he or she is. Then have the other student in the pair read the card's verse from the Bible. The first student should read the card again to reinforce the understanding of the verse.

WHAT TO DO, CONTINUED

5. Before moving on to the next pair, discuss the verse with the students to make sure they understand it.
6. When all eight of the cards have been read and discussed, have volunteers read Matthew 5:11-12 out loud to the class.

4

I want to know more about God and His will for my life. I want others around me to know about God, too.

Read Matthew 5:6

5

I am merciful. When I see people in need, I help them. When someone has wronged me, I forgive that person and do not make the person feel guilty.

Read Matthew 5:7

6

I do not like to hear bad language or watch violent movies. I do my best not to sin. I think about godly things.

Read Matthew 5:8

7

I do not hold grudges against others. I do not take part in stirring up trouble with others. I try to get along with everyone, even my enemies.

Read Matthew 5:9

8

Others do not want me to love God or follow His ways. Some say I am wrong for believing in God. I stand strong against these things.

Read Matthew 5:10

Soap Verse on a Rope

craft

WHAT YOU NEED

- duplicated page
- soap bars
- twine or rope
- toothpicks
- scissors
- glue

WHAT TO DO

1. Give each student a pattern page and an unwrapped soap bar.
2. Have the students use toothpicks to etch the words "Pure in Heart" on the plain (non-branded) sides of their soap bars.
3. Help each student cut a two-foot length of twine. Show how to tie one end around each end of the soap (about 1 inch in from the edges), to form a hanger.
4. Say, **Soap reminds us of cleanliness, or pureness. Jesus wants us to be pure in heart.**

group

WHAT YOU NEED

- pages 40 and 41, duplicated
- scissors
- tape
- yarn (optional)

WHAT TO DO

1. Give each student both pattern pages.
2. Have the students cut and fold the boxes, then tape the sides together.
3. Have the students stand in an open area. Allow time for them to shower each other with blessings by tossing around the boxes. Let them pick up thrown boxes and continue throwing until you say, "Stop!"
4. If the boxes are destroyed, allow the students to make more to take home. Option: let each student attach one box to each end of a one-foot length of yarn to hang over a doorknob.
5. Say, **Jesus will shower us with blessings when we show our beautiful attitudes!**

beatitudes

Showers of Blessing

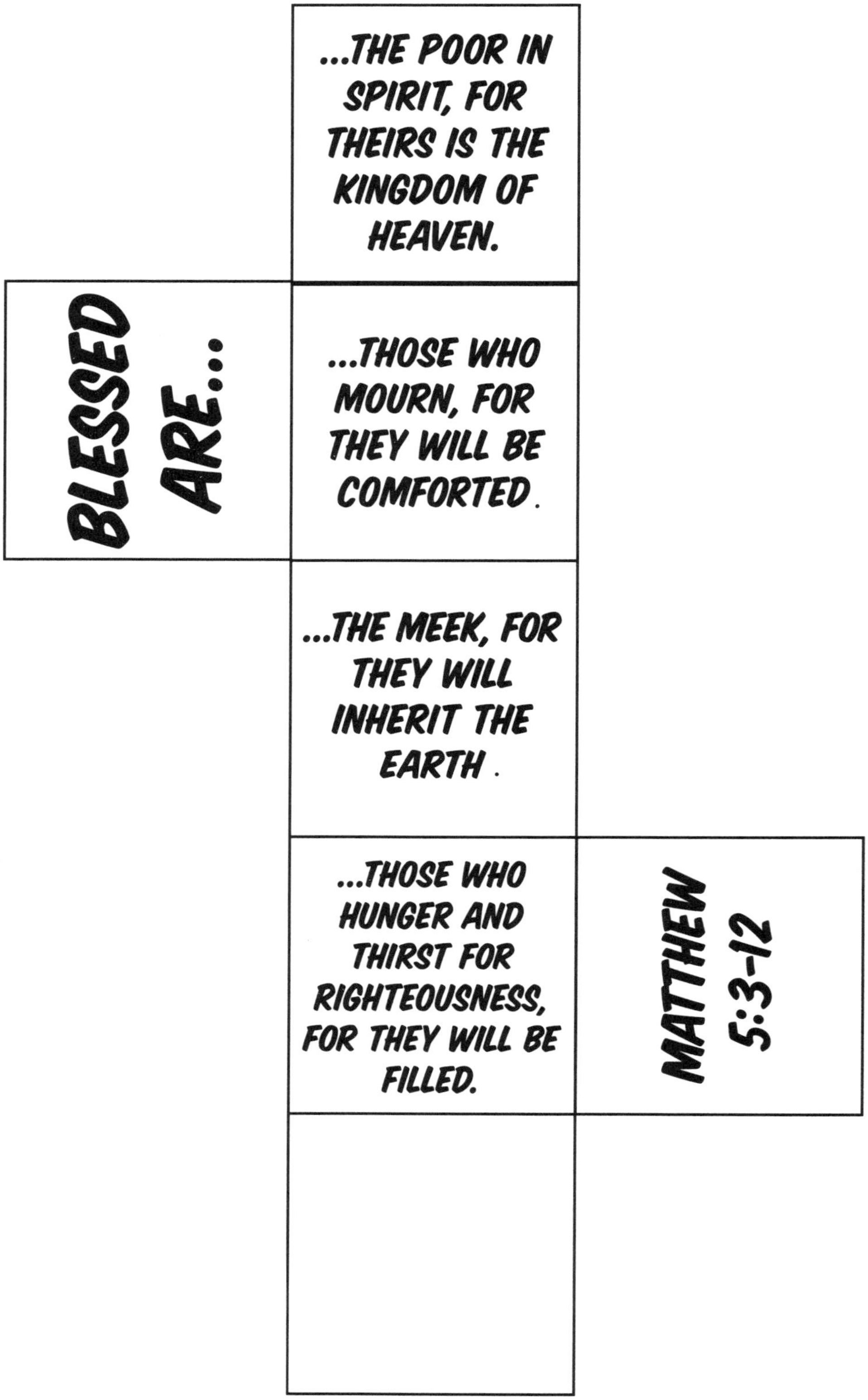

...THE POOR IN SPIRIT, FOR THEIRS IS THE KINGDOM OF HEAVEN.
BLESSED ARE...
...THOSE WHO MOURN, FOR THEY WILL BE COMFORTED.
...THE MEEK, FOR THEY WILL INHERIT THE EARTH.
...THOSE WHO HUNGER AND THIRST FOR RIGHTEOUSNESS, FOR THEY WILL BE FILLED.
MATTHEW 5:3-12

...THE MERCIFUL, FOR THEY WILL BE SHOWN MERCY.

BLESSED ARE...

...THE PURE IN HEART, FOR THEY WILL SEE GOD.

...THE PEACEMAKERS, FOR THEY WILL BE CALLED SONS OF GOD.

...THOSE WHO ARE PERSECUTED BECAUSE OF RIGHTEOUSNESS, FOR THEIRS IS THE KINGDOM OF HEAVEN.

MATTHEW 5:3-12

craft

WHAT YOU NEED

- duplicated page
- spiral or bound notebooks, 8" x 10"
- bright-colored paper
- scissors
- tape
- markers

WHAT TO DO

1. Give each student a pattern page. Have each student cut out a ribbon.
2. Let the students use markers to decorate the ribbons.
3. Have each student choose a paper color to glue onto a notebook cover, and then glue his or her ribbon on top.
4. Ask for a volunteer to read the verse in the ribbon circle aloud. Say, **Try to write in your diary every day to remember that God blesses you, no matter what. For example, you can write thanks to God for your blessings, what heaven might be like or how your blessings allow you to bless others.**

beatitudes

* Blessings Diary *

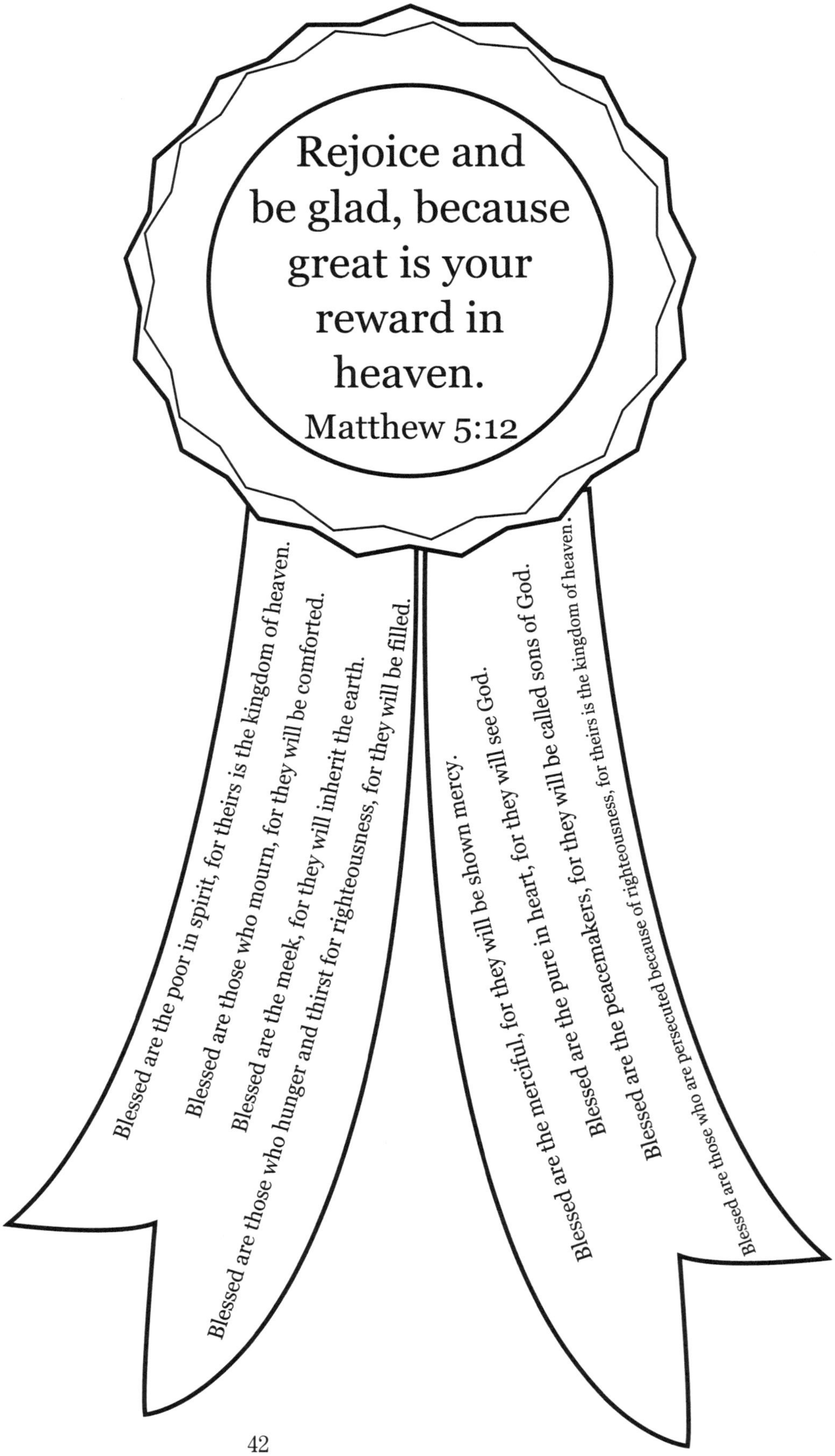

Rejoice and be glad, because great is your reward in heaven.
Matthew 5:12
Blessed are the poor in spirit, for theirs is the kingdom of heaven.
Blessed are those who mourn, for they will be comforted.
Blessed are the meek, for they will inherit the earth.
Blessed are those who hunger and thirst for righteousness, for they will be filled.
Blessed are the merciful, for they will be shown mercy.
Blessed are the pure in heart, for they will see God.
Blessed are the peacemakers, for they will be called sons of God.
Blessed are those who are persecuted because of righteousness, for theirs is the kingdom of heaven.

• CHAPTER 5 •

The Lord's Prayer

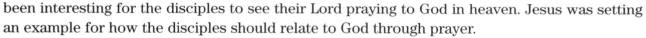

MEMORY VERSE

Our Father in heaven, hallowed be your name, your kingdom come, you will be done on earth as it is in heaven. Give us today our daily bread. Forgive us our debts, as we also have forgiven our debtors. And lead us not into temptation, but deliver us from the evil one.

MATTHEW 6:9-13

* Prayer 101 *

The New Testament gospels include many mentions of Jesus praying. It must have been interesting for the disciples to see their Lord praying to God in heaven. Jesus was setting an example for how the disciples should relate to God through prayer.

One day after watching Jesus pray, one of the disciples said, "Lord, teach us to pray."

Jesus gave His disciples this prayer to say: "Our Father in heaven, hallowed be Your name, Your kingdom come, your will be done on earth as it is in heaven. Give us today our daily bread. Forgive us our debts, as we also have forgiven our debtors. And lead us not into temptation, but deliver us from the evil one."

Jesus wanted the disciples, and us, to understand that prayer is very important. He did not intend for this prayer—what we now call "The Lord's Prayer"—to be the only prayer. But His prayer is a perfect model because it includes praise and requests for needs and forgiveness.

This prayer is included in two New Testament books: Matthew and Luke. After telling about Jesus' prayer, Matthew wrote that Jesus also explained to the disciples that they should forgive others.

In his version, Luke added that Jesus told the disciples how to ask God for what they need. "Ask and it will be given to you," Jesus said. "Seek and you will find; knock and the door will be opened to you."

God wants to hear from you. Try using the Lord's Prayer as a model of praise, petition, and forgiveness to help you form your own prayers.

BASED ON MATTHEW 6:9-15 AND LUKE 11:1-4

? Discussion Questions

1. Why do you think Jesus put praise to God first in His prayer?
2. Which part of the Lord's Prayer—praise, petition, forgiveness, or help—do you find the most difficult? Which part is easiest for you?

group

WHAT YOU NEED

- pages 44 and 45, duplicated
- pens or pencils
- Bibles

WHAT TO DO

1. Give each student the copied pages.
2. Say, **The Lord's Prayer is a model we can use to pattern our own prayers to God.**
3. Have the students read the phrases from Part A out loud. They should discuss each phrase as a class and decide which line of the Lord's Prayer it describes, then write that phrase number on the blank line beside each verse.
4. After they finish this part of the activity, say, **Now use the model prayer to write your own prayer to God on the blank lines.** Allow volunteers to read their prayers to the class, or perhaps during a planned prayer time.

prayer

Break It Down

PART A

1. Pledge to forgive others

2. Ask that God's will be done

3. Ask for God's help in avoiding the devil and his ways

4. Ask for what we need

5. Ask for forgiveness

6. Ask God to keep us from temptation

7. Recognize God as our Father in Heaven

8. Praise God

PART B

Write your own prayer using the model Jesus gave us.

Recognize God as our Father:

____

Praise God:

____

Ask that God's will be done in your life:

____

Ask for what you need:

____

Ask for forgiveness for the wrong things we do:

____

Pledge to forgive others:

____

Ask God to keep us from temptation:

____

Ask God to help us avoid the devil and his sneaky ways:

____

Any other praises to or requests for God:

____

group

WHAT YOU NEED

- duplicated page

WHAT TO DO

1. Give each student a duplicated page.
2. Have the students read the Lord's Prayer as a round by saying one word each of the Lord's Prayer. Go around the group until the entire prayer has been said aloud.
3. Practice this activity until the students can recite the entire Lord's Prayer smoothly.
4. Also explain to the students the importance of memorizing the Lord's Prayer. Say, **The more you recite this prayer over and over, the better you will learn it. Not only will you soon know a prayer you can say anytime; you are memorizing Jesus' words in Scripture!**

prayer

Round and Round

Our Father in heaven, hallowed

be your name, your kingdom

come, your will be done

on earth as it is in

heaven. Give us today our

daily bread. Forgive us our

debts as we have also

forgiven our debtors. And lead

us not into temptation, but

deliver us from the evil one.

Which One Belongs?

Circle the word that best fits with the meaning in the Bible.

Our ________ in heaven,

Enemy God Clown Daisy

________ be your name,

Ignored Funny Boring Holy

Your ________ come,

Eternity Clouds Park Property

Your ________ be done,

Demands Wants Purpose Choice

On earth as it is in ________.

Jupiter House Paradise Store

Give us today our daily ________.

Cash Food Sourdough Croissant

Forgive us our ________,

Sins Money Work Mistakes

As we also have ________ our debtors.

Blamed Hated Loved Pardoned

And lead us not into ________,

Parties Flying Testing Walking

But deliver us from ________. *—Matthew 6:9-13*

Friends Satan Singers Bikers

puzzle

WHAT YOU NEED

- duplicated page
- pens or pencils

WHAT TO DO

1. Give each student a puzzle page.
2. Say, **You have been studying and memorizing the Lord's Prayer. But do you know what it means? Look at the prayer shown. Next to each line of the Lord's Prayer are four words. Circle the word that means the same thing as the real word in the prayer.**
3. After they are finished with the puzzle, have the students read the Lord's prayer with the new words, then have them read the original prayer. Discuss any parts they do not understand.

prayer

God
Holy
Eternity
Purpose
Paradise
Food
Sins
pardoned
testing
Satan

* Napkin Basket *

craft

WHAT YOU NEED

- duplicated page
- craft foam (or cardboard)
- greeting card box bottoms (5" x 7")
- staplers
- rulers
- pencils
- scissors
- markers
- glue
- paper napkins

WHAT TO DO

1. Give each student a pattern page and a sheet of craft foam.
2. Have each student use a ruler to mark two 7¼" x 4" rectangles on a craft foam sheet and cut them out.
3. Show how to staple the two foam rectangles on each long side of the box.
4. Have each student color and cut out a Lord's Prayer shape from a pattern page, then staple the shape to one of the foam pieces.
5. Say, **Place the napkin basket on your table at home to remember the model prayer that Jesus gave us.**

prayer

The Lord's Prayer
Matthew 6:9-13

Our Father in heaven,
hallowed be your name,
your kingdom come,
your will be done
on earth as it is in heaven.
Give us today our daily bread.
Forgive us our debts,
as we have also forgiven our debtors.
And lead us not into temptation,
but deliver us from the evil one.

finished craft

* Ask, Seek, * Knock Sign

ASK AND IT WILL BE GIVEN TO YOU

SEEK AND YOU WILL FIND

KNOCK AND THE DOOR WILL BE OPENED

finished craft

craft

WHAT YOU NEED

- duplicated page
- plastic canvas sheets (13" x 10")
- foil gift wrap
- scissors
- paper fasteners
- yarn or cord
- pencils
- glue

WHAT TO DO

1. Give each student a pattern page.
2. Have the students color and cut out the shapes, then set them aside.
3. Instruct each student to cut a piece of foil wrap slightly larger than the plastic sheet, then center the foil over the plastic.
4. Show how to turn over the welcome sign, fold the foil edges toward the center back, and tape to hold.
5. Have the students use pencils to sketch "Welcome" lightly on their foil sheets.
6. Show how to push paper fasteners from the front, through the foil and plastic canvas, ➤

WHAT TO DO, CONTINUED

➤ to spell "Welcome." Have the students bend the ends of the paper fasteners on the backs of their signs to hold the fasteners in place.

7. Have the students glue their paper shapes to their welcome signs.
8. Show how to push a paper fastener through the top left and right corners of a welcome sign and tie each end of a piece of yarn to the back of each paper fastener (before securing fastener ends) for a hanger.
9. Say, **You can hang your welcome sign at home. All who see it will know that we are welcome at God's door anytime. He wants to hear from us. Ask, seek, knock—as it says in our memory verse.**

prayer

* Prayer Diary *

express yourself

WHAT YOU NEED

- duplicated page
- colorful paper
- stapler
- markers
- pens or pencils
- glue
- scissors

WHAT TO DO

1. Give each student a pattern page.
2. Let each student choose five or more pieces of colored paper.
3. Show how to stack the paper together and turn it sideways, then fold it to make a booklet that is 8½" x 5½". Have the students staple the left edges of their books to hold the pages together.
4. Instruct each student to cut out a book cover and glue it onto his or her packet of colored pages.
5. Allow the students to color or decorate the covers of their Prayer Diaries, and the pages inside, as they wish. ➢

prayer

WHAT TO DO, CONTINUED

6. Say, **Sometimes, it is easier to write what we feel than to say it, even to God. Use your Prayer Diary to write to God. Remember that He has invited us to ask, seek, and knock. No request is too little or too tough for God. Remember, also, to write down how God answers your prayers. Reading our prayers and God's answers helps us realize how well God cares for us.**

• CHAPTER 6 •

The Armor of God

MEMORY VERSE

Put on the full armor of God so that you can take your stand against the devil's schemes.

EPHESIANS 6:11

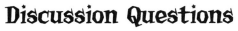

* Your Fashion Statement *

Paul wrote to the church in Ephesus to encourage them in their faith and to give them instruction on living a godly life. Our pastors do the same thing in today's churches.

Paul had something especially interesting to say to the Ephesians, however. He told them what to wear! No, it wasn't board shorts and a fun T-shirt.

Here is what Paul said: "Be strong in the Lord and in His mighty power. Put on the full armor of God so that you can take your stand against the devil's schemes."

What was this armor? It included the following:

- A belt of truth
- A breastplate of righteousness
- Feet that are ready to go share the Gospel
- A shield of faith
- A helmet of salvation
- The sword of the Spirit, which is the Word of God

Even though Paul was talking to the Ephesians, we still need these pieces of "armor" today. Truth, righteousness, readiness to spread the Gospel, faith, salvation, and knowledge of God's Word all help us to be mighty Christians, ready to fight anything that comes our way.

Imagine yourself walking around with a heavy suit of armor. Wouldn't that be silly and uncomfortable? But God's armor isn't heavy or burdensome. It is easy to wear! As you learn the important truths from God's Word, build your faith in God, tell others about His love, and stand strong against the things that would keep you from God, His armor will get lighter and lighter. Go ahead—pull on that shield and helmet!

BASED ON EPHESIANS 6:10-16

Discussion Questions

1. Why do you think Paul chose armor as a way to explain God's help in our lives?
2. Can you think of other ways, besides armor, to describe these tools God gives us?

group

WHAT YOU NEED

- duplicated page
- scissors
- poster paper
- Bibles
- tape
- glue
- crepe paper streamers
- plastic grocery bags
- flip-flop sandals
- pizza cardboard round
- fast-food bucket
- gift wrap tube
- Bible

WHAT TO DO

1. Before class, cut out the cards. Be sure to have enough armor supplies for each student to have one.
2. Create a fashion show runway in the room by taping a long sheet of paper to the floor.
3. Give each student a card. Instruct the students to put on the items listed on the cards.
4. Begin by choosing students to read Ephesians 6:10-13 aloud.
5. Have the students take their places on the runway, one at a time. Each student should "model" his ➢

armor

* Fashion Show *

Belt of Truth

Measure a one-yard length of crepe paper and glue this card to the center of it. Tie the paper around your waist.

Stand firm then, with the belt of truth buckled around your waist.
Ephesians 6:14

Breastplate of Righteousness

Slit open a plastic grocery bag to make a vest. Tape this card to it, then put it on.

With the breastplate of righteousness in place.
Ephesians 6:14

Ready Feet

Find a pair of flip-flops and put them on. Tape this card to one of them.

With your feet fitted with the readiness that comes from the gospel of peace.
Ephesians 6:15

Shield of Faith

Use a round pizza cardboard and glue this in the center.

Take up the shield of faith, with which you can extinguish all the flaming arrows of the evil one.
Ephesians 6:16

Helmet of Salvation

Tape this card on a bucket. Put the bucket on your head like a hat.

Take the helmet of salvation.
Ephesians 6:17

Sword of the Spirit

Find a cardboard gift wrap tube and tape this card to it.

And the sword of the Spirit, which is the word of God.
Ephesians 6:17

WHAT TO DO, CONTINUED

➢ or her armor and read the verse printed on the card. Make this a fun activity, and let the students overact their "modeling" if they want.

6. After the fashion show is finished, have volunteers read verses 13-17 again to put the "armor of God" pieces in the correct order in students' minds. Discuss each piece of armor to be sure the students understand what each one means.

Pennant Verse Garland

Be strong in the Lord and in his mighty power.	**Put on the full armor of God, so that you may be able to stand your ground.**
Stand firm then, with the belt of truth buckled around your waist.	**With the breastplate of righteousness in place.**
With your feet fitted with the readiness that comes from the gospel of peace.	**Take up the shield of faith, with which you can extinguish all the flaming arrows of evil.**
Take the helmet of salvation.	**Take the sword of the Spirit, which is the word of God.**

bulletin board

WHAT YOU NEED

- pages 53 and 54, duplicated
- yarn or twine
- scissors
- tape
- glue

WHAT TO DO

1. Make two copies of this page and eight copies of page 54 for each student or group.
2. Have the students cut out the phrase boxes. Each student/group will have two sets.
3. Have the students cut out the fold-over pennants.
4. Cut a three-yard length of yarn or twine for each student or group.
5. Have the students fold the pennant shapes in half. Show how to space the pennants evenly over the yarn or twine, and tape the sides of each pennant shape together. The students also should place a piece of tape at the folded edge of

armor

WHAT TO DO, CONTINUED

each pennant to hold it in place on the yarn.

6. The students should tape or glue the phrase boxes to the pennant shapes (putting matching phrases on the front and back of each pennant).
7. Say, **Let's hang our garlands around the room so we can remember the pieces of God's armor.**

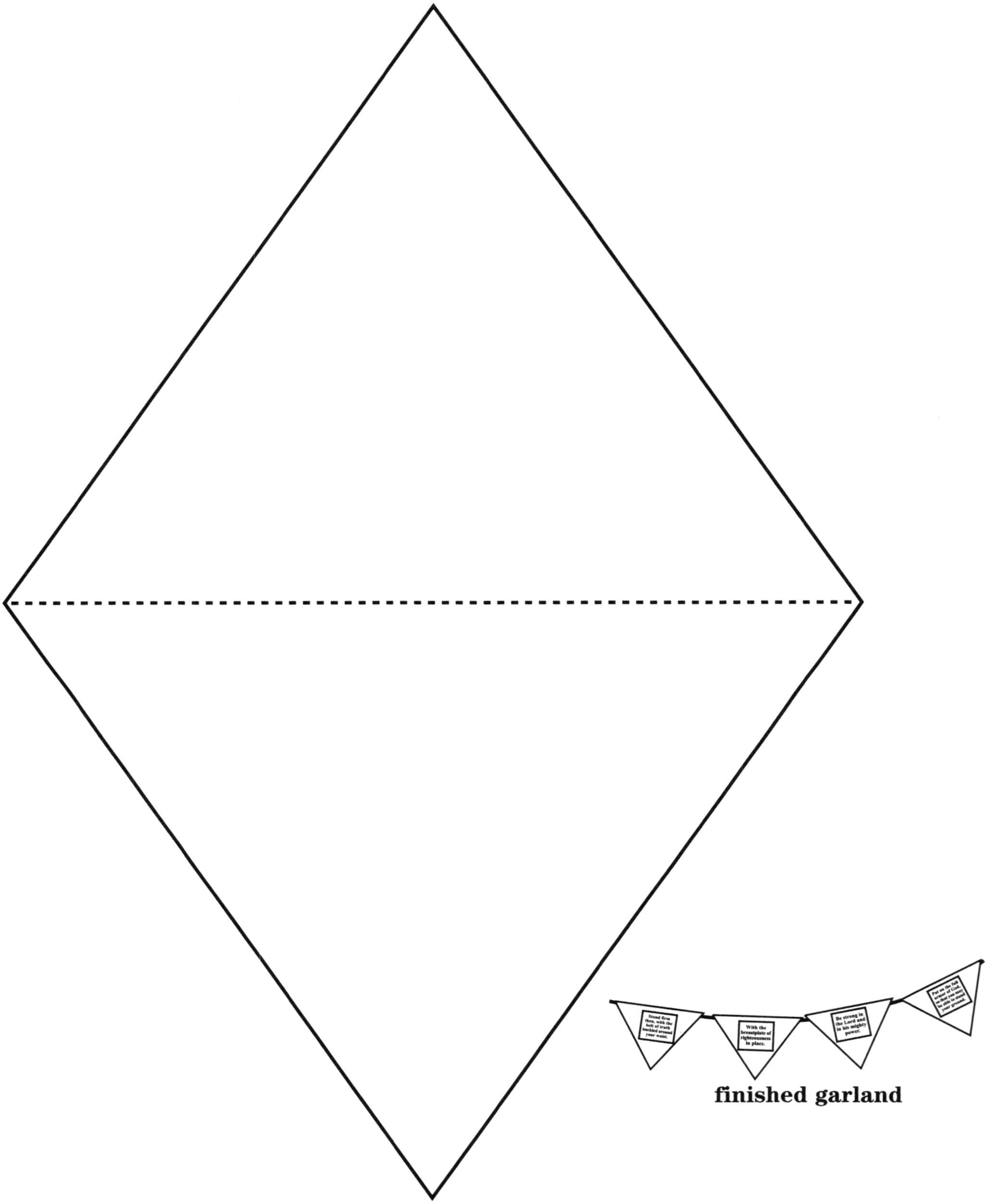

finished garland

Before and After

1. Be ___ ___ ___ ___ ___ ___
- Missing letter in Holy ___pirit
- Last letter in "spirit"
- Second letter in "prayer"
- Letter that comes after N
- Letter that comes before O
- Missing letter in "Lord ___od"

2. Wear the ___ ___ ___ ___ ___
- Say the alphabet backwards. What is the last letter you said?
- Third letter in the word "Lord."
- Missing letter in God Al___ighty
- We can extinguish the flaming arr___ws of the evil one
- Wear the belt of t___uth

3. Our struggle is against the forces of ___ ___ ___ ___
- Fit your fe___t with readiness of the gospel of peace
- On your head, you will wear the helmet of sal___ation
- Letter that comes after H in the alphabet
- Put on the ful___ armor of God

4. ___ ___ ___ ___ in the Spirit
- Wear the breast___late of righteousness
- Carry the swo___d of the Spirit
- Wear the belt of truth around your w___ist
- Second to last letter in the alphabet

5. Be ___ ___ ___ ___ ___
- Take up the shield of f___ith
- On your head, wear the he___met of salvation
- Wear the b___lt of truth
- Fit your feet with ___eadiness
- Letter after S in the alphabet.

6. Always keep on ___ ___ ___ ___ ___ ___ ___
- Letter before Q in the alphabet
- Letter after Q in the alphabet
- Put on the full ___rmor of God
- Letter before Z in alphabet
- Sh___eld of faith
- Sta___d your ground
- Wear the armor of ___od

puzzle

WHAT YOU NEED
- duplicated page
- pens or pencils
- Bibles

WHAT TO DO
1. Give each student a puzzle page.
2. Let the students work in groups. Have the groups try to solve the puzzle words.
3. When all the groups are finished, have volunteers read Ephesians 6:10-12. Say, **These verses come before those that tell us how to dress in the armor of God.**
4. Have a volunteer read Ephesians 6:18. Say, **This verse follows Paul's explanation of the armor of God.**
5. If time allows, have the students take turns reading the verses from Ephesians 6:10-18, while their minds are still focused on the word clues and the "before and after" verses.

* Armor of God Charms *

craft

WHAT YOU NEED

- pages 56 and 57, duplicated
- shrink art sheets
- scissors
- permanent markers
- toothpicks
- plastic lacing
- oven or toaster oven

WHAT TO DO

1. Give each student the two pattern pages and a shrink art sheet.
2. Have the students put the clear shrink art sheets over the pattern pages and trace each of the charms.
3. Let the students color and cut out the charms.
4. Show how to use a toothpick to poke a hole in the top of each charm.
5. Use shrink art directions to shrink the charms in an oven or toaster oven.
6. After the charms have cooled, let the students thread the charms onto lengths of plastic lacing. They can use the finished ➢

armor

WHAT TO DO, CONTINUED

➢ projects as charm necklaces, bracelets, key holders, or room or car mirror decorations.

7. Say, **These symbols will remind us to put on the "full armor of God" so we are able to stand strong for Him.**

   Note: A good substitute for the shrink art method of this project is to simply cut pieces from plastic milk jugs and have the students trace the items onto the milk jug plastic. (They don't have to be "shrunk" to make suitable charms.)

SHIELD OF FAITH
HELMET OF SALVATION
READY TO SPREAD THE GOSPEL
SWORD OF THE SPIRIT/GOD'S WORD

Verse Poster

bulletin board

WHAT YOU NEED

- pages 58 and 59, duplicated
- markers or colored pencils
- silver duct tape
- plastic tape, color variety
- scissors

WHAT TO DO

1. Duplicate the posters onto card stock or heavy paper.
2. Have the students cut shapes from silver duct tape and stick the shapes onto the armor of God pieces.
3. Have the students cut pieces from the colorful tape and stick the tape onto the current clothes pieces.
4. Say, **The armor of God will equip us to "stick" to God.**

armor

Put on the full armor of God so that you can take your stand against the devil's schemes. For our struggle is not against flesh and blood, but against the rulers, against the authorities, against the powers of this dark world and against the spiritual forces of evil in the heavenly realms. Therefore put on the full armor of God, so that when the day of evil comes, you may be able to stand your ground, and after you have done everything, to stand. Stand firm then, with the belt of truth buckled around your waist, with the breastplate of righteousness in place, and with your feet fitted with the readiness that comes from the gospel of peace. In addition to all this, take up the shield of faith, with which you can extinguish all the flaming arrows of the evil one. Take the helmet of salvation and the sword of the Spirit, which is the word of God.

Ephesians 6:11-17

• CHAPTER 7 •

Love Never Fails

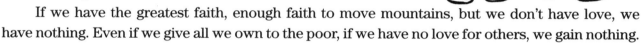

MEMORY VERSE

And now these three remain: faith, hope and love. But the greatest of these is love.

1 CORINTHIANS 13:13

* Faith, Hope, and Love *

Paul wrote to the church at Corinth to praise them for living well for God and to give them further instructions. He said he wanted to tell them "the most excellent way" to live.

If we have great gifts but no love, Paul said, we have nothing.

If we have the greatest faith, enough faith to move mountains, but we don't have love, we have nothing. Even if we give all we own to the poor, if we have no love for others, we gain nothing.

What is the link between these three? Love! Paul wanted the Corinthians (and us!) to know that we are nothing for God if we do not have love for others.

Then Paul went on to tell exactly what love looks like:

Love is patient, love is kind.

It does not envy. It does not boast. It is not proud.

It is not rude. It is not self-seeking. It is not easily angered. It keeps no record of wrongs.

Love does not delight in evil, but rejoices with the truth.

Love always protects, always trusts, always hopes, and always perseveres.

Love never fails.

Just think about how many things in your daily life that these teachings cover. We all experience times when we are impatient with others, unkind, and rude. We all have times when we are jealous of others. We all like to brag about our accomplishments, even when we hurt other people's feelings by doing so. We all show pride in things that are God's doing instead of ours.

But love does not do these things. Love doesn't delight in doing evil. Love always protects, trusts, hopes, and keeps trying to do better. Love never fails!

BASED ON 1 CORINTHIANS 12:31–13:13

Discussion Questions

1. Why do you think Paul wanted to tell the Corinthians about love?
2. How do you show love? How do people show love to you?

group

love

* Even When *

VERSES

1. Love is patient, even when [vs. 4]

2. Love is kind, even when [vs. 4]

3. Love does not envy, even when [vs. 4]

4. Love does not boast, even when [vs. 4]

5. Love is not proud, even when [vs. 4]

6. Love is not rude, even when [vs. 5]

7. Love is not self-seeking, even when [vs. 5]

8. Love is not easily angered, even when [vs. 5]

9. Love keeps no record of wrongs, even when [vs. 5]

10. Love does not delight in evil but rejoices with the truth, even when [vs. 6]

11. Love always protects, even when [vs. 7]

12. Love always trusts, even when [vs. 7]

13. Love always hopes, even when [vs. 7]

14. Love always perseveres, even when [vs. 7]

15. Love NEVER fails, even when [vs. 8]

WHAT YOU NEED

- pages 62, 63, and 64, duplicated
- scissors
- glue
- index cards
- Bibles

WHAT TO DO

1. Before class, cut page 63 into strips. Glue each situation to an index card. Leave page 62 intact.
2. Pass out the index cards to the students. Each student should have more than one card.
3. Begin by saying, **In the book of 1 Corinthians, Paul wrote to the church at Corinth to praise them for living well for God, and also to give them further instruction in godly living. Paul writes about living with love, and calls it "the most excellent way." He goes on to tell us how to live in love. Paul's teaching helps us to know** ➢

WHAT TO DO, CONTINUED

➢ **how to live in love even when we don't feel we can.**

4. Read the verses, one at a time. Say the number for each verse phrase. Then have the student with the cards for each number take turns reading the situations out loud.
5. When all the verses and situations have been read, have the students open their Bibles to 1 Corinthians 12:31–13:1-13. Ask for volunteers to read the verses.
6. Allow time for discussion of the situation cards in relationship to the Bible verses.
7. Allow students to offer their own "even when" situations.

1. Even when I'm in a hurry to meet my friends and my mom wants me to watch my little brother.

1. Even when I am so excited about the team tryouts that I can barely pay attention to my teacher.

1. Even when the person next to my locker takes forever to get out of my way.

2. Even when my neighbor yells at me for cutting across his lawn to get home.

2. Even when I have just enough to buy that CD I want, and someone I know doesn't have lunch money.

2. Even when my parents volunteer my family to help at a homeless shelter that is creepy to me.

3. Even when it seems my older sister gets everything she wants and I hardly get anything I ask for.

3. Even when someone else gets to play the solo in the band concert, and I was counting on doing it.

3. Even when that kid in my class brags about having more than some of us have.

4. Even when I beat out the star of the team for a starting position in the big game.

4. Even when I easily get A's and my friend struggles to get C's in school.

4. Even when I get to do something my brother or sister doesn't get to do.

5. Even when I won the math or spelling contest for the whole district.

5. Even when I finally did something better than my friend, and he/she always teases me when I don't do well.

5. Even when I finally have something I can use to hurt my sister's feelings.

6. Even when there's someone who is always rude to me.

6. Even when the store clerk falsely accuses me of trying to steal something.

6. Even when my parents' friend is rude at our house.

7. Even when I know I can get a good grade on the test if I don't study with my usual study-buddy.

7. Even when I feel I can be more popular if I can shame my mom into buying me expensive clothes.

7. Even when I can be in the popular crowd if I just dump my life-long friend.

8. Even when my brother lost my favorite CD.

8. Even when I feel my parents are unfair in not letting me go to a party with older kids.

8. Even when the teacher gives me a bad grade for a writing assignment just because he/she doesn't agree with my beliefs about God.

9. Even when my friend never pays me back the money he/she borrows.

9. Even when my dad disappoints me every time he promises to spend time with me.

9. Even when someone at school brags about copying my homework many times.

10. Even when someone finally gets even with the class bully.

10. Even when a teacher gets in trouble for cursing in class.

10. Even when someone tries to involve me in gossip about a kid who has spread rumors about me or someone I care about.

11. Even when I don't feel I deserve God's protection and love.

11. Even when I don't feel someone deserves my prayers or help.

11. Even when protecting someone from hurtful words will make me seem "not cool" to my classmates.

12. Even when I think my problems are too big for God.

12. Even when I feel I've done something so bad that God will never want to help me.

12. Even when I feel I can't trust anyone around me.

13. Even when I feel there's no hope for me. After all, I'm just a kid.

13. Even when the world around me seems hopeless.

13. Even when my best friend moves away and stops returning my text messages.

14. Even when my family has been hurt by people in the church, and I don't feel I can go there anymore.

14. Even when my problems wear me down and make me want to give up.

14. Even when I just can't understand math or another subject in school, and feel I may as well stop trying and just fail the class.

15. Even when I feel I have failed God.

15. Even when I feel everyone around me has failed me.

15. Even when someone tries to convince me that God doesn't love me.

*Verse Poster *

And now I will show you the most excellent way. Love is patient, love is kind. It does not envy, it does not boast, it is not proud. It is not rude, it is not self-seeking, it is not easily angered, it keeps no record of wrongs. Love does not delight in evil but rejoices with the truth. It always protects, always trusts, always hopes, always perseveres. Love never fails. And now these three remain: faith, hope and love. But the greatest of these is love.

1 Corinthians 12:31; 13:4-8, 13

bulletin board

WHAT YOU NEED

- duplicated page
- markers or colored pencils
- transparency sheets
- permanent markers
- tape

WHAT TO DO

1. Duplicate a poster onto a transparency sheet for each student.
2. Have the students color the transparency with permanent markers.
3. Tape the transparencies in a large window of your church building so everyone can enjoy the colorful "stained glass."

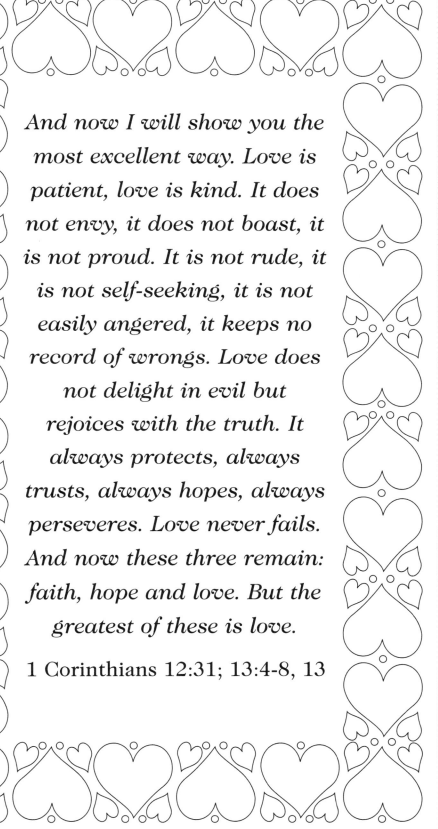

craft

WHAT YOU NEED

- duplicated page
- craft foam, various colors, including red and pink
- scissors
- pin backings
- hot/cool glue gun
- pencils or pens

WHAT TO DO

1. Give each student a pattern page.
2. Have the students choose colors of craft foam.
3. Instruct each student to cut out a hand and heart, then use pens or pencils to trace the hand onto the craft foam and cut it out.
4. They should trace and cut the heart pattern from red or pink foam.
5. Show how to fold down the middle finger and ring finger on the hand (the "love" sign).
6. Help the students use a glue gun to secure the two fingers to the hand, and glue the heart at the base of the palm (so that it doesn't overlap the folded fingers). ➢

love

Sign of Love Pin

finished craft

WHAT TO DO, CONTINUED

7. ➢ Also help each one use a glue gun to fasten a pin backing onto the back of the hand.
8. Say, **You can wear your Love Pins on a shirt, hat, or backpack to remember that love is the "most excellent way."**

Most Excellent Snack

group

WHAT YOU NEED

- duplicated page
- crispy rice cereal
- mini marshmallows
- margarine
- red food coloring
- large bowl
- large wooden or plastic spoon
- wax paper or foil
- microwave oven
- measuring cups
- plastic sandwich bags (optional)

WHAT TO DO

1. You will need access to a sink and towels, or have a dishpan of soapy water and paper towels in the classroom. Depending on your class size, have enough supplies on hand to make one or more batches of the snack.
2. Begin by having the students wash and dry their hands.
3. Guide the students as they follow the recipe to make the snack mixture.
4. Have the students rub margarine onto their hands.

Most Excellent Snack Recipe

Makes 6 heart-shaped snacks.

¼ cup margarine
6 cups crisp rice cereal
6 cups miniature marshmallows
a few drops of red food coloring

1. Place marshmallows and margarine in a large, microwave-safe bowl.
2. Cook on medium for 1 minute. Stir with spoon. Cook on medium at 20-second intervals until the marshmallows look puffed-up.
3. Add a few drops of red food coloring to the marshmallow mixture. Stir well.
4. Add more food coloring if you want the mixture darker pink or red.
5. Add cereal. Stir until cereal is well-coated with the marshmallow mixture.
6. Use about ⅙ of the mixture to form each heart shape on wax paper or foil.
7. Let the heart snacks set up firmly before eating or wrapping.

WHAT TO DO, CONTINUED

5. Place a piece of wax paper or foil on the table for each student. Give each student enough mixture for at least one heart.
6. Say, **Use the mixture to form a heart. While you're making your heart snacks, remember that the Bible says love is "the most excellent way."**
7. Let the hearts cool before the students enjoy their snacks, or have them place the snacks in plastic sandwich bags to take home.
8. The students also can take home the recipe to make the snacks with their families.

love

Perpetual Love Calendar

craft

WHAT YOU NEED

- pages 68 and 69, duplicated
- card stock
- magnet sheets, 8" x 10"
- scissors
- rulers
- markers
- stickers

WHAT TO DO

Note: This calendar will also work with felt sheets, which are less expensive than the magnetic sheets, but the months and numbers will not stick quite as well as they do with magnetic sheets.

1. Duplicate both pattern pages onto card stock for each student. Cut sheets of magnetic paper into quarters, one quarter per student.
2. Give each student both duplicated pages and a magnet sheet. Have the students cut calendar frames from the card stock.
3. Have each student glue a magnetic quarter-page inside the marked area of ➢

love

Love, the Most Excellent Way

1 Corinthians 13:1-13

WHAT TO DO, CONTINUED

➢ his or her calendar frame. The students can use markers and/or stickers to decorate the outside areas of their frames.

4. Instruct the students to cut the 12 month-strips and the 12 number sections from the second pattern page.
5. Show how to glue a piece of magnet to the back of each of the month-strips and number sections.
6. Say, **A perpetual calendar is one that can be used year after year. It doesn't expire like yearly calendars do. This calendar will remind us that our love for God and others should never expire since God's love for us will never expire! Love is "the most excellent way."**

January

February

March

April

May

June

July

August

September

November

December

October

1 2 3

4 5 6

7 8 9

0 1 2

puzzle

Color-by-Symbol

WHAT YOU NEED

- duplicated page
- colored pencils or markers

WHAT TO DO

1. Give each student a puzzle page.
2. Say, **Follow the color-by-symbol code to find the three important words in the design. Color each shape the correct color according to the symbol. Some of the letters have more than one symbol, so you will have to color half one color and half another.**
3. Have someone read the three revealed words. Have the class recite the memory verse together.

Praying hands symbol = blue

Heart symbol = red

Jesus symbol = purple

love

• CHAPTER 8 •

The Fruit of the Spirit

MEMORY VERSE

Since we live by the Spirit, let us keep in step with the Spirit.

GALATIANS 5:25

* Spirited Living *

Sin is around us every day. Things like hatred, jealousy, selfishness, fits of rage, envy, and fighting are just some of the sins Galatians 5 warns us to avoid.

But Christians have the gift of God's Holy Spirit to guide us through our daily lives. The Holy Spirit is part of the Trinity, along with God and Jesus. So the Holy Spirit is God's way of nudging you toward His will. Have you ever heard God "talking" to you about something you should or shouldn't do? That probably was the Holy Spirit doing God's work!

The Holy Spirit guides us in two ways. First, it helps us stay away from sin. As human beings, we never will be able to avoid all sin, but if we live by the Spirit, we can keep regular sin from creeping into our lives. We can rely on the Spirit to lead us on the correct paths.

Second, the Holy Spirit also produces good things in our lives. Galatians calls these good things "fruit." Who doesn't like a good piece of juicy, sweet fruit? The same can be said of these Fruits of the Spirit: love, joy, peace, patience, kindness, goodness, faithfulness, gentleness, and self-control. Who wouldn't want to have those good things in his or her life?

Listen for the Holy Spirit in your life. The more you pray and talk with God about living for Him, the more you will develop the Fruit of the Spirit.

BASED ON GALATIANS 5:16-26

Discussion Questions

1. How has the Holy Spirit helped you?
2. Which Fruit of the Spirit do you need to work on in your life?

group

WHAT YOU NEED

- duplicated page
- plain paper
- markers
- pretzel sticks
- plastic sandwich bags
- felt pieces
- glue
- permanent markers
- index cards
- eggs
- bowls
- disposable wipes
- straight pins

WHAT TO DO

1. Before class, set up the learning centers. The items needed for each center are listed. Write on an index card or piece of paper the name of the fruit that will be demonstrated at each center.
2. Have the students go to each center as a class. Have someone read the card that tells which fruit of the Spirit they will experience at that center. Tell the students what they are to do at that center, and why.
3. After the class has visited all of the ➢

fruit

Learning Centers

Love
provide paper and markers
Make a card to give someone to express your love and appreciation for him or her.

Joy
no materials needed
Sing a song together to praise God. (Suggestion: I Have the Joy, Joy, Joy Down in My Heart)

Peace
provide paper and pens
Make a pact with your class to promote peace together. Write a pledge to not argue or gossip. Post the pledge on the bulletin board or on the classroom wall where all can see it.

Patience
provide a bag of pretzel sticks and plastic sandwich bags
Count all the pretzels in a bag. Then divide the number of pretzels by the number of students in the class. Then put pretzels for each student in separate bags. Then enjoy some pretzels together.

Kindness
provide pieces of felt, permanent markers, glue
Make simple puppets for a younger class in the church. Fold pieces of felt in half, and glue the top and side seams, leaving the bottom seams open. Use permanent markers to draw facial features. Take the puppets to a kids' class.

Goodness
provide index cards and pencils
Play charades. On index cards, write some things that are good (movie, food item, sports, game, etc.). Make 10 cards. Play charades as a group.

Faithfulness
provide plain paper and markers
Make a prayer or Bible-reading chart. Use markers and plain paper to design a chart to keep track of prayer time or Bible-reading.

Gentleness
provide an egg for each student, straight pins, bowls, wipes
Try to blow the insides out of an egg without breaking the egg. Put a pinhole in the top and bottom of an egg, then gently blow through one hole to make the egg yolk and whites come out the bottom of the egg. This takes patience and great gentleness!

Self-control
no materials needed
Gather into groups of 3 or 4. Make up and perform skits about a time when one of you lost control. Repeat until everyone's embarrassing moments are acted out. Discuss ways to keep from losing control.

WHAT TO DO, CONTINUED

➢ centers, have the students take turns reading all the verses from Galatians 5:16-26. Discuss any concepts the students don't seem to understand.

Verse Poster

But the fruit of the Spirit is love, joy, peace, patience, kindness, goodness, faithfulness, gentleness and self-control. Against such things there is no law. Those who belong to Christ Jesus have crucified the sinful nature with its passions and desires. Since we live by the Spirit, let us keep in step with the Spirit. Let us not become conceited, provoking and envying each other.

—Galatians 5:22-26

bulletin board

WHAT YOU NEED

- duplicated page
- markers or colored pencils
- wallpaper samples, about 12" x 18"
- markers
- clear, self-stick plastic
- scissors
- glue

WHAT TO DO

1. Duplicate the posters onto colorful paper.
2. Have each student choose wallpaper pieces, one for each member of his or her family, and a copied poster in a color that matches the wallpaper pieces.
3. Allow the students to color the posters.
4. Have the students glue their posters in the centers of their wallpaper pieces, then cover the fronts and backs of their place mats with clear, self-stick plastic.

fruit

puzzle

WHAT YOU NEED

- duplicated page
- pens or pencils

WHAT TO DO

1. Give each student a puzzle page.
2. Say, **There are nine fruits of the Spirit in Galatians 5:22-23. See if you can find the words in the word search puzzle. Some of the words are tangled together. Some are backward or at angles. Some may go around corners. You can look in the Bible to find the words if you need them.**
3. Have the students recite the nine "fruit of the Spirit" words after they have completed their puzzles. As a reminder, fruits of the Spirit are love, joy, peace, patience, kindness, goodness, faithfulness, gentleness and self-control.

fruit

* Tangled Words *

M	R	I	S	F	G	W	K
L	S	J	R	A	A	J	D
J	R	I	W	I	A	J	K
D	O	E	R	T	S	W	Q
O	G	D	H	H	R	T	S
K	P	L	U	F	E	W	E
P	I	N	E	U	C	L	X
Z	J	N	K	L	N	R	T
Y	C	V	D	N	E	S	S
H	G	R	D	E	I	X	E
I	L	O	Z	L	T	T	L
J	O	Y	K	T	A	E	F
G	V	C	M	N	P	W	C
H	E	C	A	E	P	X	O
R	T	U	I	G	L	X	N
B	V	D	R	L	O	R	T

Rebus Story

envying

conceited

provoking

It was a bad day at school. Tasha, who always acts , stuck her nose in the air when she walked past Alison, Haley, and me. Jeremy, who is always  someone to see if he can make them angry, put his foot out and tripped Tasha. Tasha fell right on her face.

"I guess that'll teach her not to act so ," Jeremy said.

Mr. Anderson, our Christian school principal, saw the whole thing. He rounded up the group of us, including  Tasha, and herded us like a bunch of cattle into his office.

"Jeremy," Mr. Anderson said, then cleared his throat and started again. "Jeremy, I am disappointed to see you  others. Tasha could have been hurt."

"She fell right on her  face," Alison said with a giggle.

Tasha snorted. "Alison is always 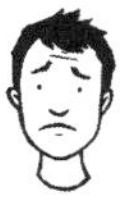 me. Her clothes look like hand-me downs. Mine are designer. Jeremy and the rest of them are always  what I have, too. All this group is constantly  me because I don't invite them to ride home in my dad's new sports car or let them come swimming in our backyard pool."

The whole group giggled and made snorting noises to mock Tasha.

"There you go again," Mr. Anderson said. " Tasha is not how we act as Christians. And you, Tasha. It seems to me that you are acting 

puzzle

WHAT YOU NEED

- page 75 and 76, duplicated

WHAT TO DO

1. Give each student a copy of the story.
2. Have the students look at the word key. Explain the words "conceited," "provoking," and "envying."
3. Have the students take turns reading the exaggerated story.
4. When they are finished, have someone read the verse from Galatians 5:26 one more time.
5. Allow time for the students to discuss their feelings about this verse and how they can keep from doing those things.

fruit

because you feel you are better than the others. Maybe they are not  you as much as you want them to."

"Yeah," Jeremy said. "  Tasha thinks we are always  her. What we really want is for her to stop treating us like we aren't good enough to be her friends."

The others agreed.

Mr. Anderson opened his desk drawer and pulled out a Bible. "Jeremy," he said, "because you seem to be the one  this whole mess, I want you to read this Scripture out loud."

Jeremy took the Bible, puffed out his chest, and read, "Galatians 5:26 – Let us not become  ,  and  each other."

Jeremy hung his head. "I'm sorry for  you, Tasha," he said.

Tasha looked at the group. "I'm sorry for acting  . I'm new at this school and don't have any friends."

The rest of us apologized, too. Alison admitted to  Tasha "just a little" for all the nice things she had.

"Hey," Tasha said. "How about you all come to my house Saturday for a swimming party?"

Everyone agreed.

"Good," Mr. Anderson said. "Now we can stop all this acting  and  each other and  . Right?"

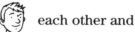

"Right," everyone said together.

Fruit of the Spirit Game

love | joy | patience

peace | kindness | goodness

faithfulness | gentleness | self-control

game

WHAT YOU NEED

- duplicated page
- card stock
- cardboard insert from 24-pack soda box (with imprints)
- scissors
- glue
- index cards

WHAT TO DO

1. Before class, cut the cardboard insert to make a playing board with nine circles, like a tic-tac-toe board. Copy the pattern page on four sheets of card stock, then cut out the "fruit of the Spirit" circles. Glue one circle inside each of the nine circles on the playing board. Cut index cards in half –you will need 21 halves. Glue 21 "fruit of the Spirit" circles onto the index cards.
2. Divide the class into two groups, or make enough games for every two students to play together.
3. To play the game,

fruit

WHAT TO DO, CONTINUED

➢ set the board on a table. Put the 21 index cards in a stack, shuffling so that the words are well mixed.

4. Player 1 should take a card from the pile and place it over the matching circle on the playing board. Then Player 2 can take a card and place it over the matching circle on the playing board. When a student draws a card that is like one already played on the board, that card gets put under the stack of cards and not played.
5. Allow the students to play the game until one person or team makes a line on the board with cards, as in tic-tac-toe.

Living by the Fruits

craft

WHAT YOU NEED

- duplicated page
- plastic or metal ring, 4" diameter
- ribbon, various colors
- craft foam
- markers
- stapler or glue
- scissors

WHAT TO DO

1. Have each student cut a gingerbread shape from a pattern page, trace it 10 times onto craft foam, and cut out the shapes.
2. Instruct the students to write the fruits of the Spirit on nine of their gingerbread shapes, one fruit per shape. On their tenth shape, they should write "The Fruit of the Spirit, Galatians 5:22-23."
3. Have each student cut five lengths of ribbon at various lengths, but each at least 2 feet long.
4. Show how to fold each ribbon in half and tie it over the bottom half of a ring, using a loop- ➣

fruit

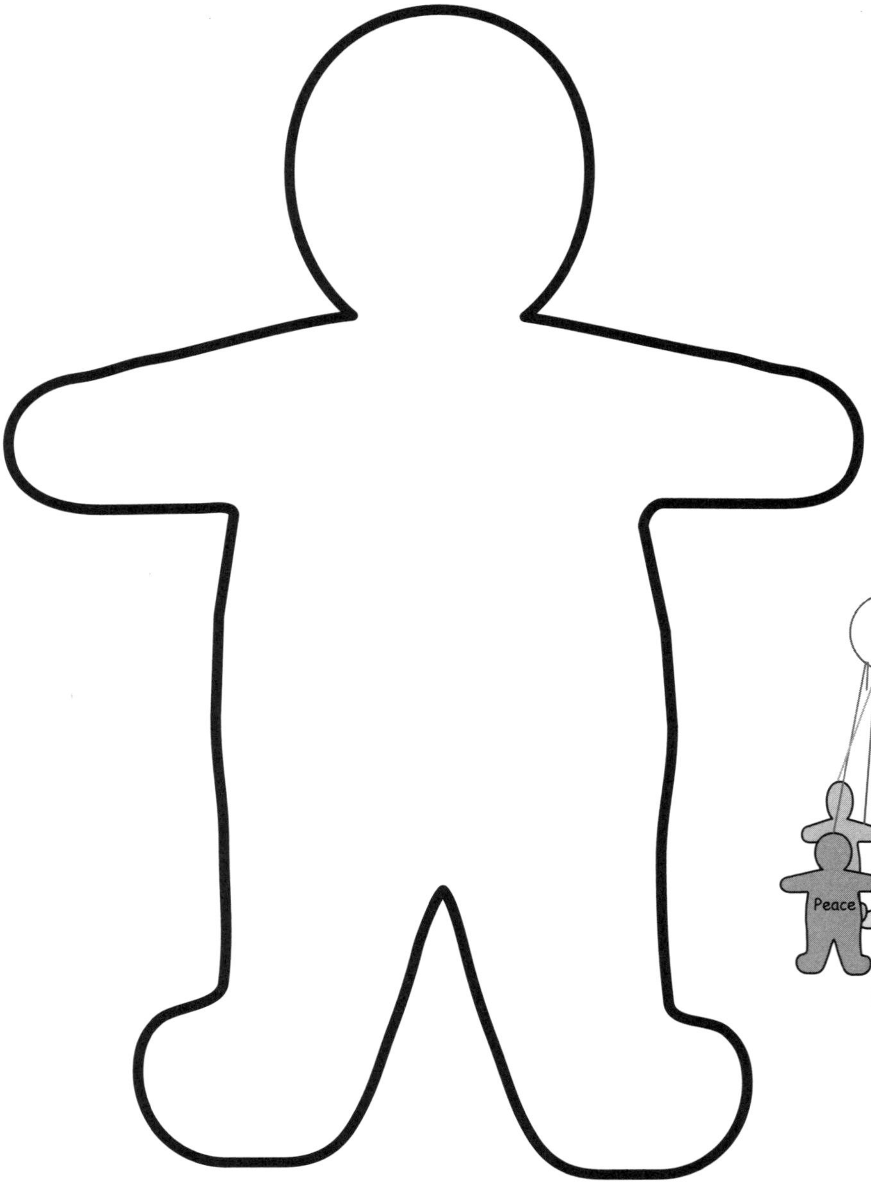

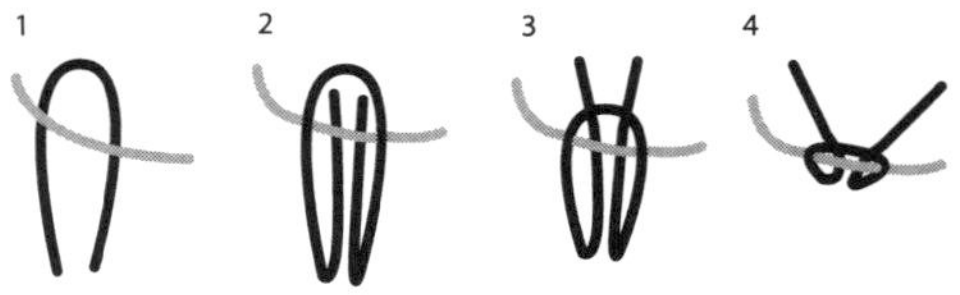

WHAT TO DO, CONTINUED

➣ knot (see illustration).

5. Have the students staple or glue their gingerbread shapes to the ribbons' ends.
6. Say, **You can post your door hanging on a door or wall at home. Each of the shapes shows a way we can live by the Spirit of God.**

* Fruit of the * Spirit Bowling

love
joy
peace
patience

game

WHAT YOU NEED

- pages 79 and 80, duplicated
- 10 dish soap bottles
- glue
- scissors
- vinyl ball

WHAT TO DO

1. Before class, cut the 10 rectangles from the two pattern pages. Glue one rectangle to each of the 10 dish soap bottles.
2. Set up the bottles in a bowling pin pattern.
3. Have the students take turns bowling with a vinyl ball. Each student must pick up the pins he or she knocks over, and read the fruits of the Spirit from each.
4. If you have a large class, make extra bowling sets.

bowling pins

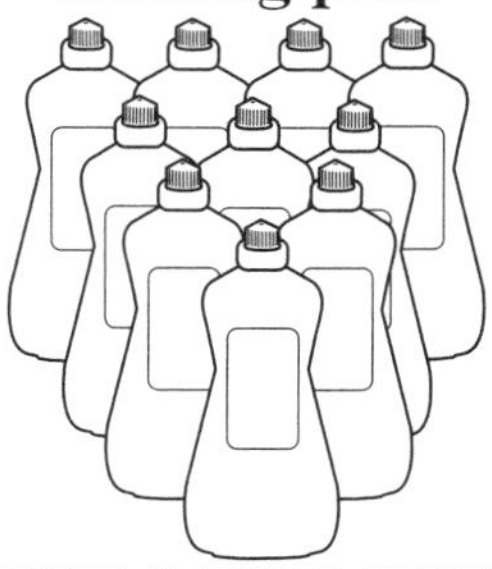

fruit

kindness

gentleness

goodness

self-control

faithfulness

Fruit of the Spirit
Galatians 5:22-23

* More Activities *

EQUIPPED WITH THE WORD OF GOD
THE GREATEST OF THESE IS LOVE

teacher help

WHAT YOU NEED

- pages 81, 82, and 83, duplicated

WHAT TO DO

These pages of clip art can be used in a variety of ways:

1. Use the art and borders for bulletin boards (enlarged), letters to parents, church bulletins, or newsletters.
2. Copy the art to plain paper. Let the students place shrink-art paper over the pictures of their choice and trace them. The students can color them with markers and shrink them in a toaster oven for jewelry, backpack tags, zipper pulls, or key chains.
3. Copy the art to white and colored paper. Let the students choose pictures to cut out and add to their scrapbooks or journals.
4. Make greeting cards for the students to send or take to nursing ➤

more

WHAT TO DO, CONTINUED

➤ home residents, shut-ins, parents, another class, or someone who is ill. Duplicate the pages, then cut out some of the artwork to copy onto sheets of paper, and quarter-fold them into greeting cards. The students can add copy with markers.

5. Enlarge the borders to use as bulletin board borders. The students will enjoy coloring the borders with markers as you share a lesson.

SWORD OF THE SPIRIT
HOLY BIBLE

LOVE IS THE MOST EXCELLENT WAY

joy gentleness

peace love kindness

patience self-control

faithfulness goodness

express yourself

WHAT YOU NEED

- duplicated page

WHAT TO DO

1. Give this award to students for memorizing any of the verses in this book.
2. Have a ceremony to present students with certificates for each of the passages they memorized. You may present one certificate for each of the eight lessons or a separate certificate for memorizing all.

more

* Equipped Awards *

Equipped Award
name
is awarded this certificate on
date
for special achievement in memorizing the Bible passages of
Scripture Reference

Why Be Equipped?

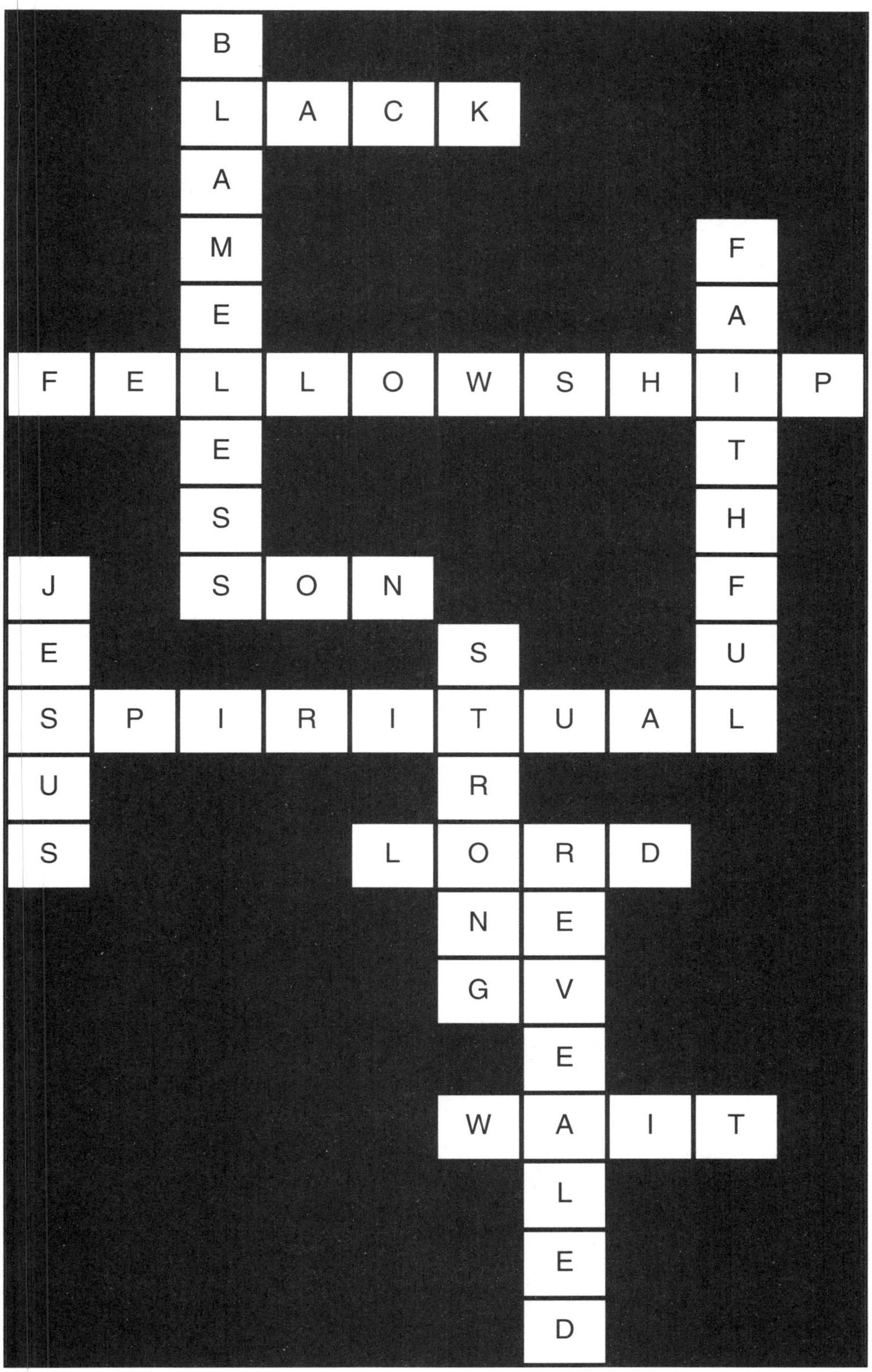

puzzle

WHAT YOU NEED

- pages 85 and 86, duplicated
- pens or pencils
- Bibles

WHAT TO DO

1. Give each student the two puzzle pages.
2. Say, **The verse we will discover in this puzzle tells us why we need to be equipped with God's Word in our hearts and minds. The backward crossword contains the words you will need to complete the verse on page 86. Some letter hints are given. Decide which word goes from the crossword to the blanks on the verse page. Write the correct words. You can cross out the words from the puzzle as you use them.**
3. When the students have finished their backward crossword puzzles, have someone read the verses aloud.

WHAT TO DO, CONTINUED

4. Allow the students to look in their Bibles for 1 Corinthians 1:7-9 to find the answers to their puzzles.

more

Therefore you do not l ___ ___ ___ any ___ p ___ ___ ___ ___ ___ ___ ___ gift as you eagerly ___ a i ___ for our ___ ___ ___ d Jesus Christ to be ___ ___ v ___ ___ ___ ___ ___. He will keep you ___ ___ ___ o ___ ___ to the end so that you will be ___ l ___ ___ ___ l ___ ___ ___ on the day of our Lord ___ e ___ u ___ Christ. God, who has called you into ___ e ___ ___ o ___ ___ ___ i ___ with his ___ ___ n Jesus Christ our Lord, is ___ ___ ___ th___ ___ ___.

—1 Corinthians 1:7-9

How-to Book

craft

How to Be Equipped to Live for God

1. How to Live Like God Wants
2. How to Know God Takes Care of All My Needs
3. How to Love God
4. How to Be Blessed
5. How to Pray
6. How to Stand Strong
7. How to Show Love
8. How to Live by the Spirit

WHAT YOU NEED

- duplicated page
- construction paper
- stapler

WHAT TO DO

1. Give each student a duplicated Table of Contents page (this page), and the eight posters duplicated from Lessons 1-8.
2. Have the students put their pages together to form books.
3. Instruct the students to cover their How-to Books with construction paper. and staple the books together at the left edges.
4. Say, **Keep your How-to Book handy, so you can review your "equipped" verses often. God wants us to be equipped with His Word.**

more

song

WHAT YOU NEED

- duplicated page

WHAT TO DO

1. Give each student a duplicated song page.
2. Have the students sing the song to the tune of "God Is So Good."
3. Say, **Keep this song in your Bible or on your bulletin board at home. It will help you remember how to be equipped for God.**

more

* Equipped *

I'm equipped to live for God,
I'm equipped to live for God,
I'm equipped to live for God,
I know the Word of God.

I know the Ten Commandments,
I know the Ten Commandments,
I know the Ten Commandments,
Exodus 20:1-17.

The Lord, my Shepherd, leads me,
The Lord, my Shepherd, leads me,
The Lord, my Shepherd, leads me,
The 23rd Psalm.

The greatest commandment says "love God,"
The greatest commandment says "love God,"
The greatest commandment says "love God,"
Deuteronomy 6:5.

The Beatitudes tell me how to be blessed,
The Beatitudes tell me how to be blessed,
The Beatitudes tell me how to be blessed,
Matthew 5:3-12.

I know the Lord's Prayer,
I know the Lord's Prayer,
I know the Lord's Prayer,
Matthew 6:9-15.

I have the armor of God,
I have the armor of God,
I have the armor of God,
Ephesians 6:10-18.

The most excellent way is love,
The most excellent way is love,
The most excellent way is love,
1 Corinthians 13:1-13.

I live by the Spirit of God,
I live by the Spirit of God,
I live by the Spirit of God,
Galatians 5:22-26.

✴ Bible Verse Spirals ✴

craft

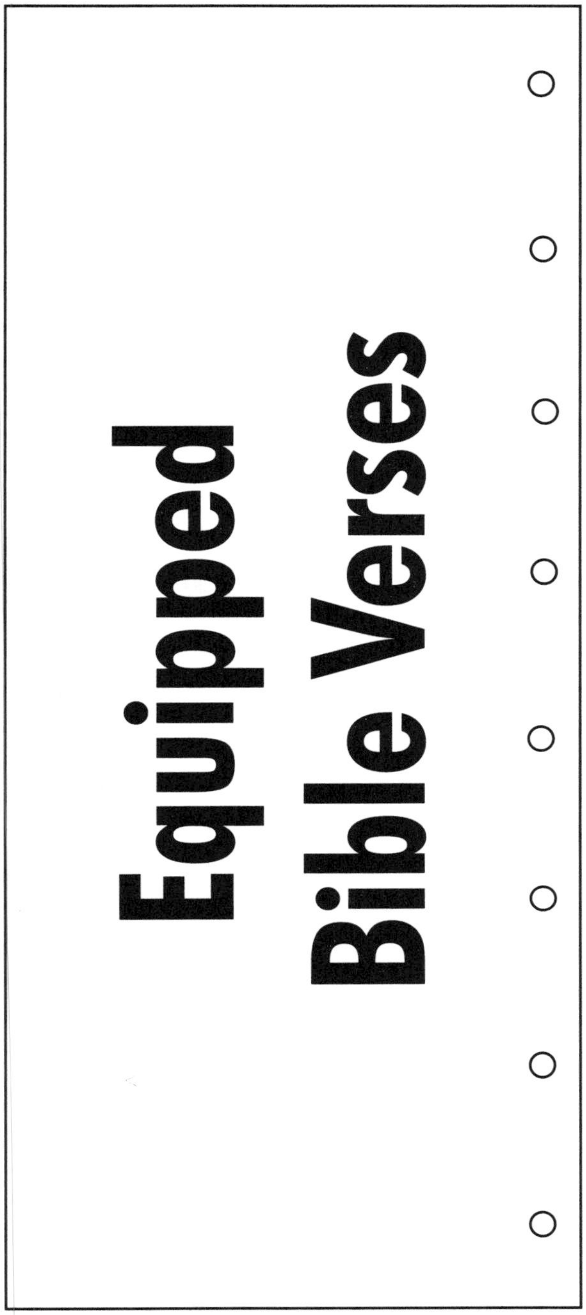

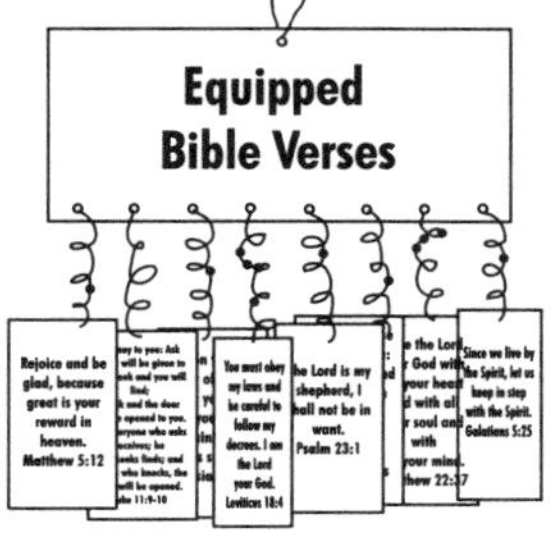

finished craft

WHAT YOU NEED

- pages 89, 90, and 91, duplicated
- card stock
- chenille stems
- craft beads, any size and color
- scissors
- tape

WHAT TO DO

1. Duplicate the pattern pages on card stock for each student.
2. Have the students cut out the "Equipped Bible Verses" rectangles and the eight verse sections.
3. Let each student choose eight chenille stems.
4. Show how to curl a stem into a spiral shape and thread a few colorful beads onto the spiral.
5. Show how to push the top edge of a stem spiral into one of the eight marked spots on the "Equipped" rectangle, then push the bottom edge of the stem spiral through the marked spot in one

➤ more

WHAT TO DO, CONTINUED

➤ of the verse sections.
6. Have each student make a hanger for his or her Bible Verse Spirals by forming a loop from a chenille stem and taping the loop to the top of the "Equipped" rectangle.
7. Say, **The Spiral Verse Hanging will remind you that God's Word equips you for life!**

Rejoice and be glad, because great is your reward in heaven. *—Matthew 5:12*	You must obey my laws and be careful to follow my decrees. I am the Lord your God. *—Leviticus 18:4*
So I say to you: Ask and it will be given to you; seek and you will find; knock and the door will be opened to you. For everyone who asks receives; he who seeks finds; and to him who knocks, the door will be opened. *—Luke 11:9-10*	Put on the full armor of God so that you can take your stand against the devil's schemes. *—Ephesians 6:11*

The Lord is my shepherd, I shall not be in want. *—Psalm 23:1*	Love the Lord your God with all your heart and with all your soul and with all your mind. *—Matthew 22:37*
And now these three remain: faith, hope and love. But the greatest of these is love. *—1 Corinthians 13:13*	Since we live by the Spirit, let us keep in step with the Spirit. *—Galatians 5:25*

• ANSWER KEY •

Equipped For Life Answer Key

Page 8: A Closer Look

1. gods
2. idol
3. jealous
4. punish
5. love; love (or obey)
6. name; guiltless
7. Sabbath
8. father; mother
9. long life
10. murder
11. adultery
12. steal
13. give false testimony
14. cover

Page 13: Message from God

"You have seen for yourselves that I have spoken to you from heaven."
—Hebrews 11:6

Page 22: Crossword Psalm

Across	*Down*
2. love	1. overflows
4. shepherd	3. table
7. follow	5. house
10. rod	6. righteousness
11. guides	8. want
12. waters	9. oil
13. forever	15. shadow
14. pastures	16. name
17. staff	20. evil
18. enemies	24. Lord
19. goodness	
23. valley	
25. soul	

• ANSWER KEY •

Equipped For Life Answer Key

Page 30: All Word Search

T	S	O	U	L	S	T	R	E	N
R	L	S	T	R	E	N	G	T	G
A	U	R	T	S	O	U	L	H	T
E	O	A	O	U	L	S	S	H	H
H	S	E	S	**H**	E	T	T	E	H
H	T	H	T	R	A	R	R	A	E
T	R	H	T	G	N	E	E	R	A
G	A	E	H	H	T	G	N	T	R
N	E	R	T	S	L	U	O	S	T

Page 34: Discover More
"And the second is like it: 'Love your neighbor as yourself.' —Matthew 22:39

Page 36: Jesus, Healer and ...
meek; mourn; peacemaker; spirit; pure in heart; hunger and thirst; merciful
Unscrambled word: teacher

Page 47: Which One Belongs?
God; holy; eternity; purpose; paradise; food; sins; pardoned; testing; Satan

Page 55: Before and After
1. Be strong
2. Wear the armor
3. Our struggle is against the forces of evil
4. Pray in the Spirit
5. Be alert
6. Always keep on praying

• ANSWER KEY •

Equipped For Life Answer Key

Page 70: Color-by-Symbol
Faith, Hope, Love

Page 74: Tangled Words

M	R	I	S	F	G	W	K
L	S	J	R	A	A	J	D
J	R	I	W	I	A	J	K
D	O	E	R	T	S	W	Q
O	G	D	H	H	R	T	S
K	P	L	U	F	E	W	E
P	I	N	E	U	C	L	X
Z	J	N	K	L	N	R	T
Y	C	V	D	N	E	S	S
H	G	R	D	E	I	X	E
I	L	O	Z	L	T	T	L
J	O	Y	K	T	A	E	F
G	Y	C	M	N	P	W	C
H	E	C	A	E	P	X	O
R	T	U	I	G	L	X	N
B	V	D	R	L	O	R	T

Page 85: Why Be Equipped?
"Therefore you do not lack any spiritual gift as you eagerly wait for our Lord Jesus Christ to be revealed. He will keep you strong to the end so that you will be blameless on the day of our Lord Jesus Christ. God, who has called you into fellowship with his Son Jesus Christ our Lord, is faithful."
—1 Corinthians 1:7-9